W9-ASR-824

004
GRA
Cıl

Graham, Ian
The world of computers and
. . .

14.85

DATE DUE	BORROWER'S NAME
Dova and	Carlos
	Jorge

004
GRA
Cıl

Graham, Ian
The world of computers and
. . .

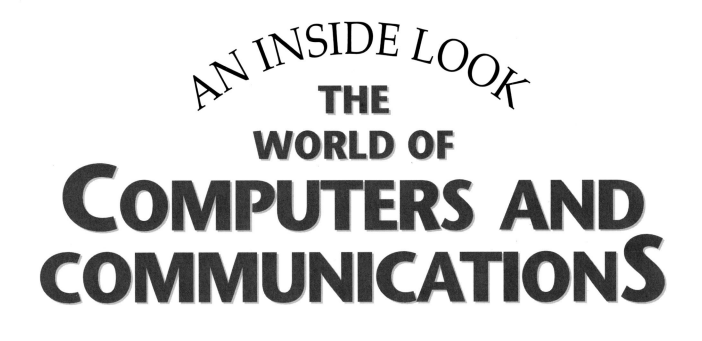

AN INSIDE LOOK

THE WORLD OF

COMPUTERS AND COMMUNICATIONS

For a free color catalog describing Gareth Stevens Publishing's
list of high-quality books and multimedia programs,
call 1-800-542-2595 (USA) or 1-800-461-9120 (Canada).
Gareth Stevens Publishing's Fax: (414) 332-3567.

The editors would like to extend thanks to Kevin Pulz,
Executive Producer/Director-Instructor, Milwaukee Public
Television, Channels 10&36, Milwaukee, Wisconsin, for his
kind and professional help with the information in this book.

Library of Congress Cataloging-in-Publication Data available upon request
from publisher. Fax: (414) 332-3567 for the attention of the Publishing
Records Department.

ISBN 0-8368-2727-9

This North American edition first published in 2000 by
Gareth Stevens Publishing
A World Almanac Education Group Company
330 West Olive Street, Suite 100
Milwaukee, WI 53212 USA

This U.S. edition © 2000 by Gareth Stevens, Inc. Original
edition © 1998 by Horus Editions Limited. First published
as *The World of Computers and Communications* in the series
How It Works by Horus Editions Limited, 1st Floor,
27 Longford Street, London NW1 3DZ, United Kingdom.
Additional end matter © 2000 by Gareth Stevens, Inc.

Illustrators: Jeff Bowles, Sebastian Quigley, and Gerald Witcomb
Gareth Stevens editors: Christy Steele and Heidi Sjostrom

Printed in Mexico

1 2 3 4 5 6 7 8 9 04 03 02 01 00

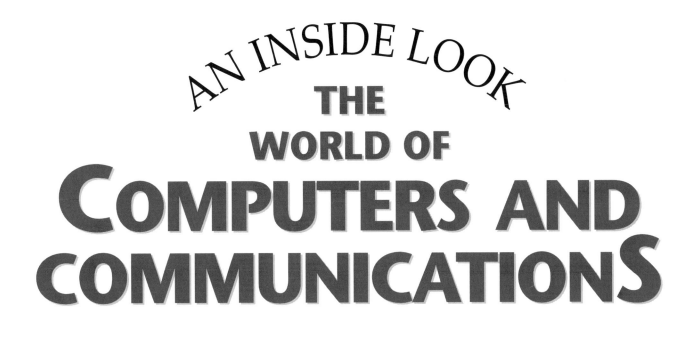

AN INSIDE LOOK
THE
WORLD OF
COMPUTERS AND COMMUNICATIONS

Ian Graham

Gareth Stevens Publishing
A WORLD ALMANAC EDUCATION GROUP COMPANY

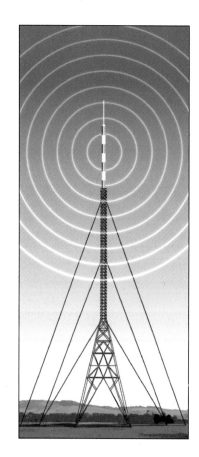

AN INSIDE LOOK

CONTENTS

Printing

People communicate with each other in many ways — by using words, sounds, facial expressions, pictures, gestures, and other means. Printing presses help make communication easier by producing many copies of words and pictures at once. Presses are printing machines that work by coating a printing plate with ink. The inked plate is pressed against paper to make the ink stick to the paper. There are three main printing methods: letterpress, lithography, and gravure. The letterpress makes the image or text on the paper by coating raised parts of the printing plate with ink. In gravure, tiny pits in the metal plate form the parts to be printed. The plate is coated with ink and then cleaned to remove all the ink, except for droplets that remain in the tiny pits. When the plate is pressed against paper, ink from the pits soaks into the paper. Litho printing — Lithography — works because water and grease separate. The part of the plate that will not be printed is wet with water so the greasy ink will stick to only the dry parts. Modern printing presses use the offset-litho printing method (*see right*).

THE GIANT ROLL OF BLANK PAPER IS CALLED A REEL.

A FAST OFFSET PRESS MAY USE 28 MILES (45 KILOMETERS) OF PAPER IN AN HOUR.

THE FIRST PRINTING UNIT USES CYAN (BLUE-GREEN) INK.

THE SECOND PRINTING UNIT PRINTS WITH MAGENTA (PURPLE-RED) INK.

THE THIRD PRINTING UNIT PRINTS WITH YELLOW INK.

THE FINAL PRINTING UNIT PRINTS WITH BLACK INK.

A COMPUTER CONTROLS THE PRESS.

Printing in color

A printing press can print any color by using only four different colors of ink. The four colors are cyan (blue-green), magenta (purple-red), yellow, and black. Four separate printing plates are made. Each color is printed on the paper separately as it makes its way through the press. The colored inks are never mixed. Instead, the four colors are printed as tiny dots, which are so small that they merge, or blend, together on the paper to make different colors. The colors depend on the size and spacing of the tiny dots.

The printing press prints the cyan part of the image first (1). Then the paper moves on to the next stage, and the magenta part is printed on top of it (2). The paper moves on again, and the yellow part is added (3). The process is completed by printing the black part (4).

①
②
③
④

A FULL-COLOR IMAGE IS PRINTED IN FOUR STAGES.

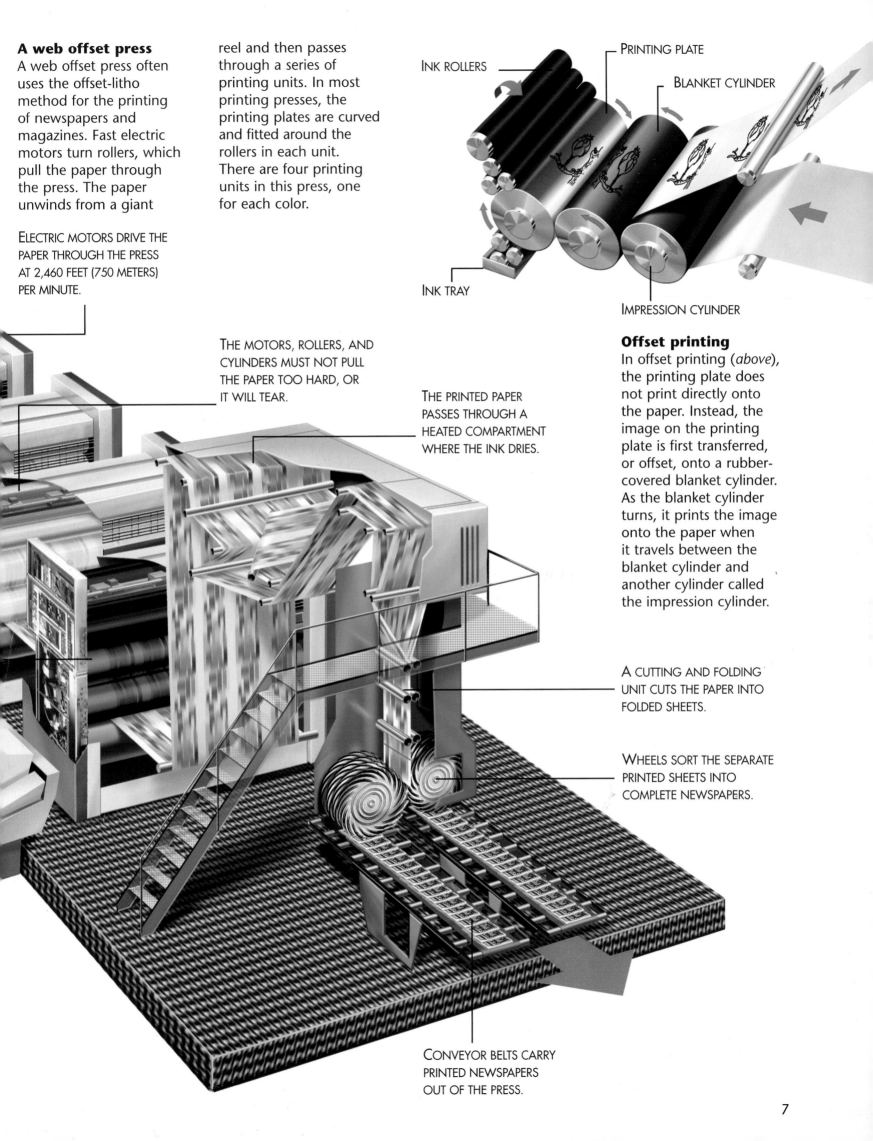

A web offset press

A web offset press often uses the offset-litho method for the printing of newspapers and magazines. Fast electric motors turn rollers, which pull the paper through the press. The paper unwinds from a giant reel and then passes through a series of printing units. In most printing presses, the printing plates are curved and fitted around the rollers in each unit. There are four printing units in this press, one for each color.

ELECTRIC MOTORS DRIVE THE PAPER THROUGH THE PRESS AT 2,460 FEET (750 METERS) PER MINUTE.

THE MOTORS, ROLLERS, AND CYLINDERS MUST NOT PULL THE PAPER TOO HARD, OR IT WILL TEAR.

THE PRINTED PAPER PASSES THROUGH A HEATED COMPARTMENT WHERE THE INK DRIES.

INK ROLLERS

PRINTING PLATE

BLANKET CYLINDER

INK TRAY

IMPRESSION CYLINDER

Offset printing

In offset printing (*above*), the printing plate does not print directly onto the paper. Instead, the image on the printing plate is first transferred, or offset, onto a rubber-covered blanket cylinder. As the blanket cylinder turns, it prints the image onto the paper when it travels between the blanket cylinder and another cylinder called the impression cylinder.

A CUTTING AND FOLDING UNIT CUTS THE PAPER INTO FOLDED SHEETS.

WHEELS SORT THE SEPARATE PRINTED SHEETS INTO COMPLETE NEWSPAPERS.

CONVEYOR BELTS CARRY PRINTED NEWSPAPERS OUT OF THE PRESS.

Taking Pictures

A camera is a machine inside a light-proof box that is used to take photographs. It has a lens at the front, film inside, and a shutter that opens to let light touch the film. The lens has an adjustable opening, or aperture, made from a circle, or diaphragm, of metal plates. When a photograph is taken, the camera's shutter opens for a fraction of a second, and the lens focuses an image of the outside world onto the light-sensitive film. The amount of light falling onto the film can be adjusted in two ways: the aperture can be widened or narrowed, or the shutter speed can be changed to lengthen or shorten the time the shutter is open. For most photographs, the shutter is open for less than one-hundredth of a second. Electronic circuits in many cameras measure the strength of light and set the aperture and shutter speed automatically.

PEOPLE PRESS THE SHUTTER-RELEASE BUTTON TO TAKE A PHOTOGRAPH.

The Single Lens Reflex

The Single Lens Reflex (SLR) is a popular type of camera. It uses a lens, a mirror, and a block of glass called a prism to form both the image on the film and the image viewed through the camera's eyepiece. This method creates the same image that is seen in the eyepiece on the photograph. Other types of cameras use two lenses, which can create different images. If the camera is not held in the right way, the image on the photograph may not match the image seen in the eyepiece.

THE SHUTTER SPEED IS SELECTED BY TURNING A DIAL TO THE DESIRED SETTING.

A SMALL, LIQUID-CRYSTAL DISPLAY SHOWS INFORMATION ABOUT THE CAMERA'S SETTINGS.

THE EYEPIECE SHOWS A VIEW OF WHAT THE CAMERA'S LENS IS POINTING AT.

ELECTRONIC CIRCUITS MONITOR AND CONTROL THE CAMERA.

BATTERIES POWER THE CAMERA'S ELECTRONIC CIRCUITS AND MOTORS.

A MOTOR PULLS OUT A NEW PIECE OF FILM FOR EACH PHOTOGRAPH.

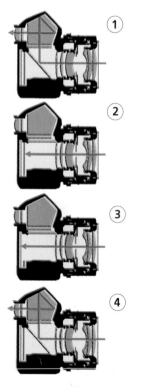

① ② ③ ④

Pressing the button

Light coming in through the lens is reflected up to the eyepiece at the top of the camera by a mirror and a block of glass called a prism (1). To take a photograph, the shutter-release button is pressed. This causes the mirror to swing up and the aperture diaphragm to adjust to the correct size (2). Then the shutter itself opens to let light fall on the film (3). Finally, the shutter closes after a set time; the mirror drops down, and the aperture diaphragm opens again to give a bright view through the eyepiece (4).

THE APERTURE IS SET BY
TURNING A RING ON THE LENS.

A PRISM REFLECTS LIGHT
COMING UP FROM THE
MIRROR TO THE EYEPIECE.

THE FILM UNWINDS FROM
A SMALL METAL CAN AS THE
PHOTOGRAPHS ARE TAKEN.

THIS DIAL SETS THE
EXPOSURE SPEED, OR
LIGHT SENSITIVITY, TO
MATCH THE FILM INSIDE.

THE ENLARGER

FILM

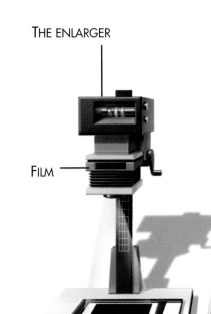

Making a photograph

First, people treat the film
from the camera with
chemicals. Then they place
the film in the enlarger.
A sheet of light-sensitive
paper is placed in a frame
underneath it. When the
enlarger light is turned on,
it projects the picture from
the film onto the paper.
The paper is then soaked
in a chemical developer,
and the picture appears.

TRAY OF DEVELOPING
CHEMICAL

THE APERTURE IS ADJUSTED
TO CONTROL THE AMOUNT
OF LIGHT PASSING THROUGH.

THE PICTURE IS FOCUSED BY
ANOTHER RING ON THE LENS.

THE LENS
COLLECTS LIGHT
AND FOCUSES IT.

ZOOM LENS AF 28-80mm 1:2.8-4.5

Freezing the action

A photograph shows
a single moment of
action that is frozen
in time. This means
photographs can show
us things that happen
too quickly for the
human eye to observe.
Here, a photograph
shows the droplets and
ripples a raindrop makes
when it falls into water.
To freeze a fast event like
this, the camera's shutter
may be open for only
one-thousandth of a
second. The picture will
be blurred if the shutter
is open for too long.

A FAST SHUTTER
SPEED CAN
FREEZE ACTION.

AN ELECTRIC MOTOR
CAN AUTOMATICALLY
FOCUS A CAMERA.

A MIRROR REFLECTS LIGHT UP
TO THE TOP OF THE CAMERA.

THE LENS IS ACTUALLY MADE
UP OF A SERIES OF LENSES.

Cameras in Space

Earth's atmosphere bends the light from objects in space in different directions. This effect makes stars appear to twinkle. Unfortunately, this effect also prevents astronomers from taking clear photographs through their telescopes. To reduce this effect, telescopes are often built on mountain tops or in other high places with less atmosphere above them. The best pictures are taken high above the atmosphere from satellite telescopes orbiting in space. The Hubble Space Telescope (*right*) is the biggest of these orbiting telescopes. Its telescope points deep into space, and cameras record the images produced. Cameras on board other orbiting satellites keep a constant watch on Earth. Cameras carried by deep-space probes have photographed the planets and many of their moons. The probes send their photographs back to Earth by radio.

THE TELESCOPE RECEIVES COMMANDS AND SENDS DATA TO EARTH USING TWO DISH-SHAPED RADIO ANTENNAE.

THE PRIMARY MIRROR IS 94 INCHES (2.4 M) ACROSS AND IS MADE FROM ALUMINUM-COATED GLASS.

THE HUBBLE SPACE TELESCOPE ORBITS EARTH AT A HEIGHT OF ABOUT 373 MILES (600 KM).

TINY HEATERS WARM THE INSTRUMENTS WHILE THE TELESCOPE IS IN EARTH'S COLD SHADOW.

THE TELESCOPE'S TWO CAMERAS ARE HELD IN HERE.

THE TELESCOPE'S IMAGE IS FORMED HERE.

THE AFT SHROUD PROTECTS THE INSTRUMENTS AND THE MIRROR INSIDE IT.

STAR TRACKERS CAN LOCK THE TELESCOPE ONTO ANY STAR AND HOLD THE TELESCOPE STEADY AND FOCUSED.

BATTERIES SUPPLY ELECTRICITY WHEN THE TELESCOPE PASSES INTO EARTH'S DARK SHADOW.

TWO WINGLIKE SOLAR PANELS GENERATE ELECTRICITY FROM SUNLIGHT.

The Hubble Space Telescope

The space shuttle launched the Hubble Space Telescope (HST) in 1990. Its primary mirror reflects starlight entering the telescope to its secondary mirror, which then reflects the light down the telescope to a package of cameras and other instruments. The HST can take much clearer photographs than telescopes on Earth because it is above the atmosphere. The fuzzy image (*below left*) shows the star Melnick 34 as seen through a telescope on Earth. The sharp, clear image (*below right*) shows the same star seen through the HST as it orbits in space.

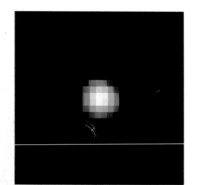

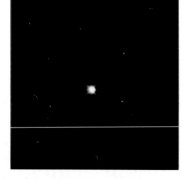

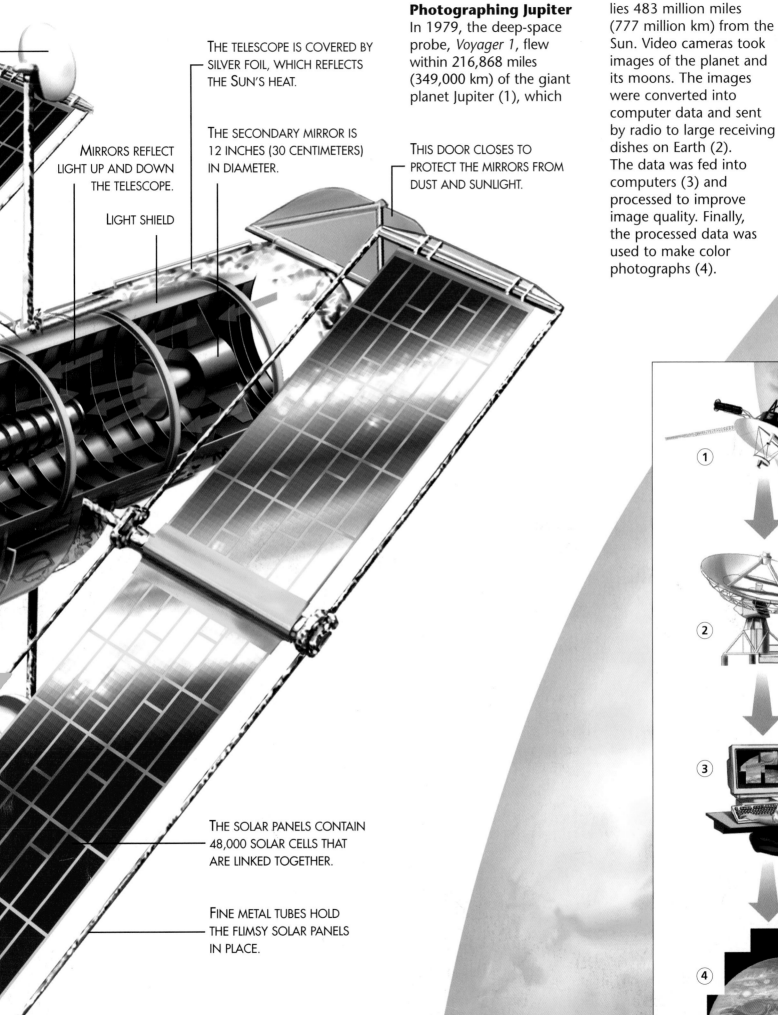

THE TELESCOPE IS COVERED BY SILVER FOIL, WHICH REFLECTS THE SUN'S HEAT.

MIRRORS REFLECT LIGHT UP AND DOWN THE TELESCOPE.

LIGHT SHIELD

THE SECONDARY MIRROR IS 12 INCHES (30 CENTIMETERS) IN DIAMETER.

THIS DOOR CLOSES TO PROTECT THE MIRRORS FROM DUST AND SUNLIGHT.

Photographing Jupiter
In 1979, the deep-space probe, *Voyager 1*, flew within 216,868 miles (349,000 km) of the giant planet Jupiter (1), which lies 483 million miles (777 million km) from the Sun. Video cameras took images of the planet and its moons. The images were converted into computer data and sent by radio to large receiving dishes on Earth (2). The data was fed into computers (3) and processed to improve image quality. Finally, the processed data was used to make color photographs (4).

THE SOLAR PANELS CONTAIN 48,000 SOLAR CELLS THAT ARE LINKED TOGETHER.

FINE METAL TUBES HOLD THE FLIMSY SOLAR PANELS IN PLACE.

TV Cameras

Television cameras turn images of the real world into electrical signals, which can be broadcast and changed back into pictures by a television set.

Modern television cameras depend on a special type of chip called a Charge-Coupled Device (CCD), which changes light into electricity. Hundreds of thousands of light-sensitive points cover a CCD. When light falls on a CCD, it changes the voltage of these points according to how bright the light is. Voltage is the force that makes an electric current flow. In a fraction of a second, electronic circuits inside the camera read the voltage at every point on the CCD. This makes an electrical copy of the picture. Other circuits add extra information to mark the beginning and end of each line of the picture and each complete picture.

The electrical signals from the camera encode and send all the pictures the camera takes. These signals can be broadcast live or recorded on videotape to be edited and broadcast later.

Inside a TV camera

Light enters a television camera through a zoom lens. Pressing a switch turns on an electric motor that adjusts the lens to make the picture bigger or smaller. Light-sensitive devices inside the camera change the pictures from light into electrical signals. The camera operator aims the camera and looks through the viewfinder to make sure the focus is correct and the picture includes what it should. A tiny television screen shows the view through the camera lens.

A MIRROR REFLECTS THE VIEWFINDER IMAGE OUT THROUGH THE EYEPIECE.

THE CAMERA OPERATOR LOOKS THROUGH THE VIEWFINDER. USUALLY, THESE DEVICES AND CONTROLS ARE ON THE CAMERA'S OTHER SIDE.

A MICROPHONE CAN BE MOUNTED ON THE CAMERA TO PICK UP SOUND.

ELECTRONIC CIRCUITS CHANGE THE SIGNALS FROM THE CCDs INTO A TELEVISION PICTURE SIGNAL.

A CUSHIONED SHOULDER PAD MAKES THE CAMERA COMFORTABLE TO HOLD.

THE OPTICAL BLOCK SENDS THREE IMAGES TO THREE SEPARATE LIGHT-SENSITIVE DEVICES.

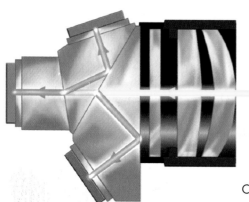

Splitting light

Light enters a television camera and passes through a specially shaped block of glass — a prism — which splits the light up into three beams. Coatings on the glass surface separate the incoming light into its red, green, and blue components. Three images (a red, a green, and a blue) fall on three CCDs. They produce the three signals that are combined by a television set to make a picture.

Satellite dish
A microwave radio dish or satellite dish beams pictures from an outside broadcast to an inside control room.

Editing computer
A computer can add captions to the pictures or mix (combine) two or more television pictures together to create effects.

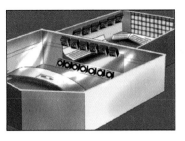

The control room
In a control room, which is usually next to a studio, the director decides which camera's view to broadcast.

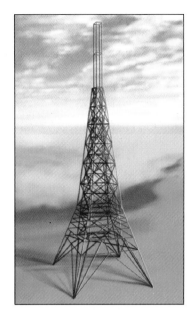

The transmitter
The studio transmits pictures and sound as radio signals. The radio signals spread out at the speed of light from the top of a transmitter tower.

THE VIEWFINDER MONITOR IS A TINY TELEVISION SCREEN.

"CAMERA-ON" INDICATOR LIGHT

LIGHT ENTERS THE CAMERA THROUGH THE LENS.

A HOOD AROUND THE LENS STOPS STRAY LIGHT FROM ENTERING THE CAMERA.

THE LENS IS MADE FROM SEVERAL LENSES WORKING TOGETHER.

EXTRA CONTROLS ADJUST THE LENS.

13

Televisions

A television set receives radio signals and changes them into sounds and pictures. The moving picture that appears on the screen really is a series of dots of light that appear quickly one after another. In a fraction of a second, the screen and our eyes combine many separate lines containing hundreds of light dots into one picture. Glowing chemicals called phosphors are painted on the back of television screens. An electron gun in the back of the television fires three different beams of electrically charged particles called electrons at the phosphors. Phosphors glow and create light when they are struck by the electron beams. The electron beams sweep back and forth across the screen, tracing out the lines of light dots. The red, green, and blue phosphors are lit up by different electron beams. By varying the strengths of the beams, the three primary colors can be combined to make a whole range of colors.

AIR CIRCULATES FREELY INSIDE THE SPACIOUS CASE.

HEAT ESCAPES THROUGH VENTILATION SLOTS IN THE CASE.

THE TV CASE CUSHIONS THE TUBE FROM DAMAGING BUMPS AND KNOCKS.

THE PICTURE IS MADE FROM TINY RED, GREEN, AND BLUE DOTS.

MODERN TELEVISION SETS HAVE FLATTER SCREENS THAN OLDER SETS.

SOME PORTABLE TELEVISION SETS USE THIN, FLAT LCD OR PLASMA SCREENS (see left).

INDICATORS LIGHT UP TO SHOW THAT THE TELEVISION IS SWITCHED ON AND IS WORKING CORRECTLY.

A PHOTO-SENSOR HIDDEN BEHIND A RED FILTER RECEIVES COMMANDS FROM THE REMOTE-CONTROL HANDSET.

A FEW ESSENTIAL CONTROLS ARE DISPLAYED IN FRONT, WHILE OTHERS MAY BE HIDDEN BEHIND A FLAP.

Television on the move

The largest part of old television sets was the glass picture tube. It was very heavy and fragile. The tube needed high voltages to send electrons at a high speed from the back of the tube to the front. However, people now build small television sets with screens that are thin, flat, lightweight LCDs (liquid crystal displays) or plasma (which works with electrically charged gas). New screens work on much lower voltages. Using batteries, they can be watched from a car, pocket, or wristwatch.

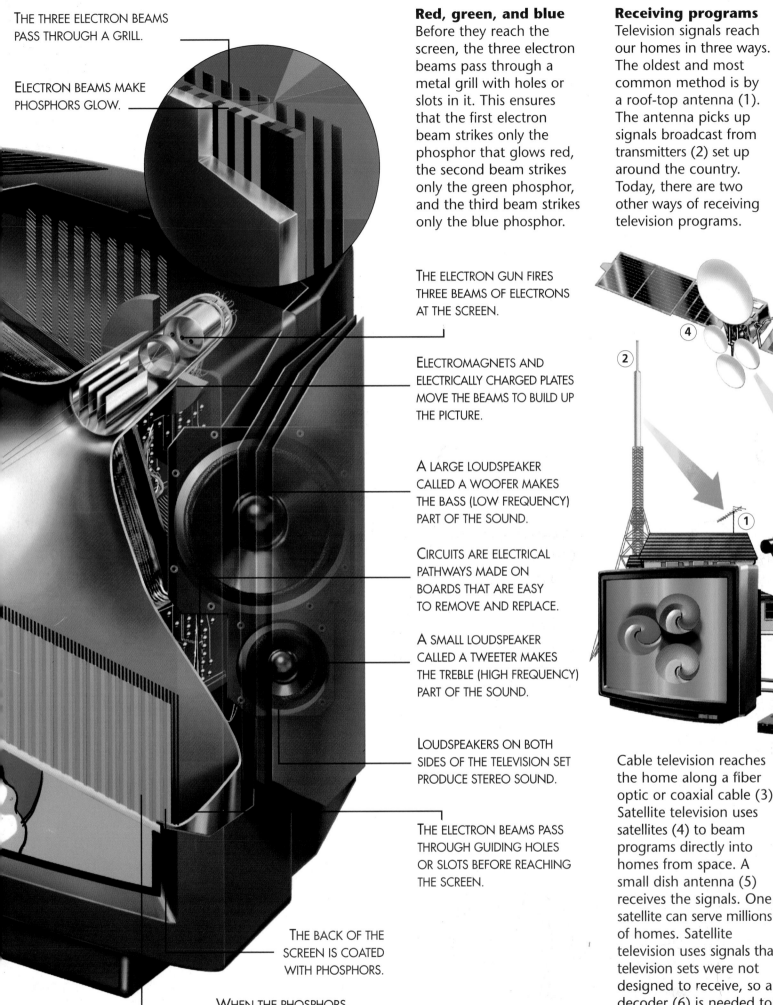

THE THREE ELECTRON BEAMS PASS THROUGH A GRILL.

ELECTRON BEAMS MAKE PHOSPHORS GLOW.

Red, green, and blue
Before they reach the screen, the three electron beams pass through a metal grill with holes or slots in it. This ensures that the first electron beam strikes only the phosphor that glows red, the second beam strikes only the green phosphor, and the third beam strikes only the blue phosphor.

Receiving programs
Television signals reach our homes in three ways. The oldest and most common method is by a roof-top antenna (1). The antenna picks up signals broadcast from transmitters (2) set up around the country. Today, there are two other ways of receiving television programs.

THE ELECTRON GUN FIRES THREE BEAMS OF ELECTRONS AT THE SCREEN.

ELECTROMAGNETS AND ELECTRICALLY CHARGED PLATES MOVE THE BEAMS TO BUILD UP THE PICTURE.

A LARGE LOUDSPEAKER CALLED A WOOFER MAKES THE BASS (LOW FREQUENCY) PART OF THE SOUND.

CIRCUITS ARE ELECTRICAL PATHWAYS MADE ON BOARDS THAT ARE EASY TO REMOVE AND REPLACE.

A SMALL LOUDSPEAKER CALLED A TWEETER MAKES THE TREBLE (HIGH FREQUENCY) PART OF THE SOUND.

LOUDSPEAKERS ON BOTH SIDES OF THE TELEVISION SET PRODUCE STEREO SOUND.

THE ELECTRON BEAMS PASS THROUGH GUIDING HOLES OR SLOTS BEFORE REACHING THE SCREEN.

THE BACK OF THE SCREEN IS COATED WITH PHOSPHORS.

WHEN THE PHOSPHORS ARE STRUCK BY ELECTRON BEAMS, THEY GLOW RED, GREEN, OR BLUE.

Cable television reaches the home along a fiber optic or coaxial cable (3). Satellite television uses satellites (4) to beam programs directly into homes from space. A small dish antenna (5) receives the signals. One satellite can serve millions of homes. Satellite television uses signals that television sets were not designed to receive, so a decoder (6) is needed to change the signals into a form that television sets can use.

At the Movies

The film for a motion picture (movie) looks like a moving picture when it is projected, but it is actually a series of still pictures on film. Each picture is slightly different from the one before. The pictures are shown one after the other so quickly that we see them as one moving picture. The pictures that appear on the screen are made by shining a light from a projector through the film. The picture is only one part of watching a movie. The sound is equally important. The latest movies have digital soundtracks with six different sound channels.

The projector
An electric motor winds film through the projector. Each picture frame is held in place for a moment and projected onto the screen by a bright light. A lens focuses the image. Then a spinning shutter cuts off the light, and the film is moved on by one more frame. The intensely bright light inside the projector creates a lot of heat. Fans constantly circulate cooler air to stop the projector from overheating.

FANS KEEP THE PROJECTOR COOL BY BLOWING HOT AIR OUT THROUGH METAL DUCTS (PIPES).

DIGITAL SOUNDTRACK

Motion picture film
Motion picture film contains both pictures and sound. The digital soundtrack is printed between the holes along one edge of the film. The soundtrack is picked up by shining a light through the edge of the film onto a photo sensor.

THE PROJECTOR'S LIGHT SOURCE IS A VERY BRIGHT LIGHTBULB.

A SILVER REFLECTOR BOUNCES LIGHT FORWARD THROUGH THE FILM TO THE MOVIE SCREEN.

THE FILM UNWINDS FROM
A SPOOL.

SHORT FILM SPOOLS ARE
ATTACHED TO THE PROJECTOR.
LONGER FILM SPOOLS ARE
MOUNTED ON A TABLE BESIDE
THE PROJECTOR.

SPRING-LOADED
ROLLERS TAKE UP ANY
SLACK IN THE FILM.

THE LENS FOCUSES
THE PICTURE.

A SPINNING SHUTTER CUTS
OFF THE LIGHT WHILE THE
FILM IS MOVING.

FILM LEAVING THE PROJECTOR
IS WOUND AROUND THE
TAKE-UP SPOOL.

The screen

The movie screen is a reflective white surface, onto which the film is projected and focused. Black blinds on each side of the screen can be moved in or out to change the shape of the screen. Most movies are shot on film 35 millimeters wide, but other film sizes (16 mm and 70 mm) are used for different effects.

Surround sound

Loudspeakers all around a theater allow sound to reach the audience from every direction. Most of the speech comes from speakers behind the center of the screen. Most of the music and background sounds come from speakers at each side of the screen. Sound effects come from side and rear speakers.

SURROUND SPEAKERS LINE THE
REAR OF THE THEATER.

LOUDSPEAKERS ARE BEHIND
THE MOVIE SCREEN.

LARGE LOUDSPEAKERS CALLED
SUB-WOOFERS PRODUCE
THE LOW BASS PARTS OF
A FILM'S SOUNDTRACK.

Tape Recording

Tapes store copies of sounds or pictures. Audiotape records only sound. Videotape records both sound and pictures. Data is recorded on thin, plastic film. The film is coated with powder made of microscopic, needle-shaped particles that can be magnetized. This magnetic recording tape is like a long, narrow ribbon. It winds around reels inside a plastic case called a cassette.

A tape or video recorder's job is to change sounds or pictures into electric currents. Then it changes the electric currents into magnetic patterns on the tape. A machine that plays the tape works in the opposite way. It changes magnetic patterns recorded on the tape back into electric currents. Then the currents are converted into sound. Most tape machines (*right*) can both record and play sounds.

Recording on tape
The magnetic particles on blank recording tape are magnetized in different directions, so they cancel out each other's magnetic force. When a tape recording is made, the recording head magnetizes the particles into regular patterns, strengthening their magnetic force.

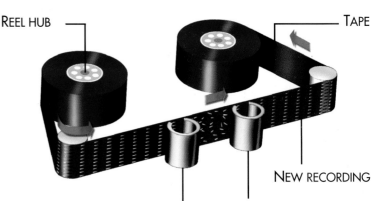

REEL HUB

TAPE

NEW RECORDING

THE ERASE HEAD REMOVES ANY RECORDING ON THE TAPE BEFORE RECORDING ON IT AGAIN.

THE RECORD/PLAYBACK HEAD MAKES A NEW RECORDING BY MAGNETIZING THE TAPE.

THE TOP OF THE PLAYER OPENS SO THAT A TAPE CASSETTE CAN BE LOADED.

BATTERIES PROVIDE ELECTRICAL POWER FOR THE MOTOR THAT DRIVES THE TAPE AND THE ELECTRONIC CIRCUITRY.

HEADPHONES ARE PLUGGED INTO THE PLAYER.

Video recording
A videocassette recorder (VCR) records sounds and pictures it receives from a television antenna. When a cassette is pushed inside the machine, a loop of tape is pulled out and wrapped around the video drum, which contains the recording and playback heads. The drum spins as the tape moves past it. One spin of the drum records or plays one television picture.

VIDEO DRUM

TV TUNER

11.30 4

EARPHONE SOCKET

THE AMPLIFIER STRENGTHENS THE ELECTRONIC SIGNALS FROM THE PLAYBACK HEAD SO THAT THEY CAN BE HEARD IN THE EARPIECES AS SOUNDS.

CONTROL PANEL

TAPE CASSETTE

CLOCK/TIMER DISPLAY

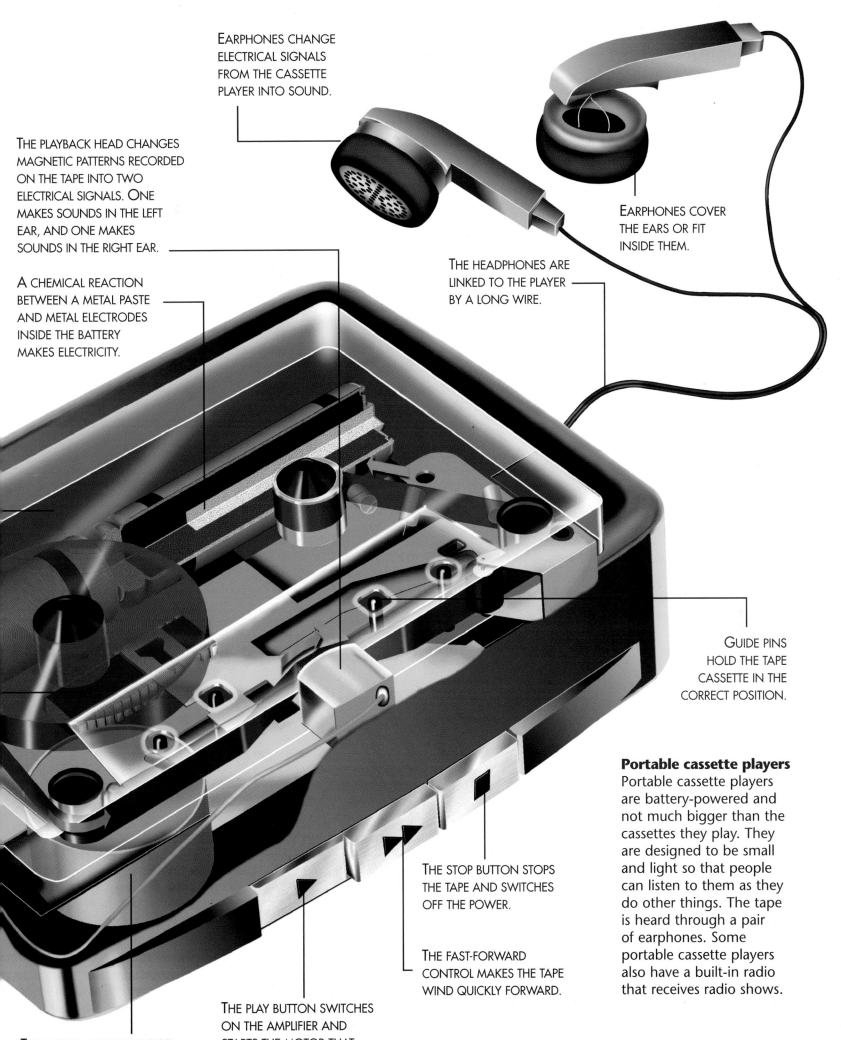

EARPHONES CHANGE ELECTRICAL SIGNALS FROM THE CASSETTE PLAYER INTO SOUND.

THE PLAYBACK HEAD CHANGES MAGNETIC PATTERNS RECORDED ON THE TAPE INTO TWO ELECTRICAL SIGNALS. ONE MAKES SOUNDS IN THE LEFT EAR, AND ONE MAKES SOUNDS IN THE RIGHT EAR.

A CHEMICAL REACTION BETWEEN A METAL PASTE AND METAL ELECTRODES INSIDE THE BATTERY MAKES ELECTRICITY.

EARPHONES COVER THE EARS OR FIT INSIDE THEM.

THE HEADPHONES ARE LINKED TO THE PLAYER BY A LONG WIRE.

GUIDE PINS HOLD THE TAPE CASSETTE IN THE CORRECT POSITION.

Portable cassette players
Portable cassette players are battery-powered and not much bigger than the cassettes they play. They are designed to be small and light so that people can listen to them as they do other things. The tape is heard through a pair of earphones. Some portable cassette players also have a built-in radio that receives radio shows.

THE STOP BUTTON STOPS THE TAPE AND SWITCHES OFF THE POWER.

THE FAST-FORWARD CONTROL MAKES THE TAPE WIND QUICKLY FORWARD.

THE PLAY BUTTON SWITCHES ON THE AMPLIFIER AND STARTS THE MOTOR THAT MOVES THE TAPE.

THE MOTOR DRIVES THE TAPE FROM ONE REEL TO THE OTHER.

Compact Discs

Compact discs (CDs) are discs used to store high-quality recorded sound. Sound is recorded on a CD as a pattern of microscopic pits. The pits are pressed into a silver-colored layer of metal. The metal is coated with a protective, clear plastic layer. To play a CD, a CD player uses an electric motor to spin the disc at high speed. A laser shines a narrow beam on the spinning disc. Reflections of the beam bounce back off the disc and are changed into electrical signals by a photo-sensor. The signals are then turned into sound. The pattern of pits in most CDs cannot be changed. Unlike a tape cassette, the standard music CD is a read-only disc. Special discs, however, are recordable.

Portable CD players

The electronic and mechanical parts of a CD player can now be made so small and light that portable CD players have become very popular. Portable CD players are available on their own or built into portable stereo systems (*above*). Portable players are often fitted with anti-shock systems, so the music continues playing, even when the player moves, and the laser is nudged out of position for a moment.

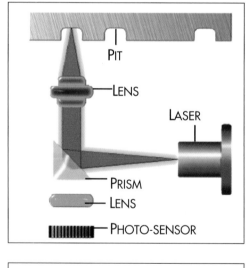

PIT
LENS
LASER
PRISM
LENS
PHOTO-SENSOR

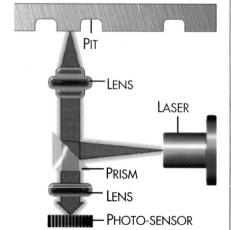

PIT
LENS
LASER
PRISM
LENS
PHOTO-SENSOR

Playing a CD

A tiny laser underneath the compact disc produces a narrow beam. A lens focuses the beam onto a tiny spot. When the laser beam lands on a pit in the disc (*left, top*), the rough surface of the pit scatters the laser beam in all directions. When the disc spins around a fraction more, the laser beam falls on its smooth silver surface (*left, bottom*). This makes a bright reflection bounce back from the disc through another lens and onto a photo-sensor. The photo-sensor changes the flashing reflections into a series of electrical pulses. The CD player then converts this stream of electrical codes into sounds you can hear.

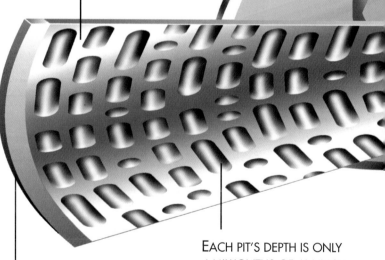

A CD SPINS FROM 200 TO 500 TIMES PER MINUTE.

MUSIC IS RECORDED ON ONLY ONE SIDE OF A CD.

THE TRACKS OF PITS ARE VERY CLOSE TOGETHER.

THE DISC IS 0.05 INCHES (1.2 MM) THICK.

EACH PIT'S DEPTH IS ONLY 4 MILLIONTHS OF AN INCH (1 TEN-THOUSANDTH OF A MM).

The compact disc

All standard CDs measure 4.7 inches (120 mm) across. Sound is always recorded on them in the same way, so a CD can be played on any CD player anywhere in the world. A standard CD can hold up to 74 minutes of sound. The tiny pits that contain the sound data are arranged in a spiral. As a CD plays, the laser moves across the disc to follow the path of the pits from the inside of the disc to its outside.

THE CD LABEL IS PRINTED ON TOP.

A PLASTIC CORE LAYER

AN ALUMINUM COATING

THE DISC SPEED VARIES TO KEEP THE TRACK SPEED AT 4 FEET (1.2 M) PER SECOND.

A CD TRACK STARTS CLOSE TO THE CENTER OF THE DISC AND SPIRALS OUTWARD.

RAINBOW COLORS APPEAR ON A CD BECAUSE THE PITS INTERFERE WITH LIGHT REFLECTIONS FROM THE DISC.

THE LASER PRODUCES AN INVISIBLE INFRARED BEAM.

THE LASER SCANS ACROSS THE DISC FROM NEAR THE CENTER TO THE OUTSIDE.

A PRISM BOUNCES THE REFLECTED LASER BEAM ONTO A PHOTO-SENSOR.

THE SILVER-LOOKING LAYER IN THE DISC IS MADE FROM THE METAL ALUMINUM.

THE PHOTO-SENSOR CHANGES LIGHT INTO ELECTRICAL SIGNALS.

Electronics

Equipment in the world of modern communications relies for its functioning on electronics. In machines that use electronics, there are devices called components, which control how electrons move in electric circuits. Electrons are invisible particles found in all atoms. Electrons produce an electrical current when they move through a material. Electrical currents used in communications carry information, such as numbers, words, sounds, or pictures. For example, currents carry voices along wires from one telephone into another telephone. The electrical currents flow around circuits and through components. Components, such as transistors and microchips, control the currents, switching them on or off or making them larger or smaller.

All modern communications depend on electrical currents and the electronic components that shape them. In this electronic security system (*right*), electrical current flowing along wires allows the main control circuit to communicate with the sensors that detect a burglar breaking into a home.

Resistor
A resistor is a component that resists the flow of electrical current. It works by changing some of the electrical energy passing through it into heat.

Transistor
Transistors are used in two ways – as switches (turning electrical currents on and off) or as amplifiers (making currents larger).

A WINDOW SENSOR IS ACTIVATED WHEN THE WINDOW OPENS.

Electrical current
An electrical current is the flow of electrons from atom to atom through a material, such as a copper wire. The more electrons that flow, the greater the current produced.

A WIRE LINKS SENSORS TO THE ALARM CIRCUIT.

ELECTRONS JUMP FROM ATOM TO ATOM ALONG THE WIRE.

SOUND WAVES

Fuse
A fuse is a thin piece of wire designed to melt if too much electrical current flows through a circuit. It reduces the risk of electric shocks or fires.

Capacitor
A capacitor can store electricity for a period of time and then release it again. Capacitors can be used to smooth out variations in voltage.

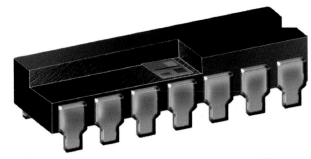

Microchip
A microchip, or integrated circuit, is a circuit constructed on a tiny sliver of silicon embedded in a block of plastic. Several microchips can be linked together to form more complex circuits, such as a computer. Different types of microchips contain different electronic circuits. The type of circuit and what it is used for depends on what sort of electronic components it contains and how they are connected together.

THE CONTROL BOX CONTAINS THE MAIN CIRCUIT BOARD.

LEDS LIGHT UP TO SHOW WHICH PARTS OF THE SYSTEM ARE SWITCHED ON.

MICROCHIPS CONTAIN MOST OF THE SYSTEM'S ELECTRONIC COMPONENTS.

ELECTRONIC COMPONENTS CHANGE THE ELECTRICAL CURRENTS FLOWING THROUGH THEM.

A BATTERY POWERS THE ALARM DURING A POWER CUT.

Light-emitting diode
A light-emitting diode (LED) lights up like a bulb when an electrical current passes through it (*left*). LEDs are used instead of bulbs because they are almost unbreakable, and they use less electricity.

Electronic alarms
Homes and businesses are often protected by electronic security systems. All the windows and doors are fitted with sensors. These are switches that are activated when a window or door opens. Rooms may also be protected by motion sensors that detect movement. If someone enters a room after the alarm has been switched on, the circuit in the main control box detects which sensors have been activated and sounds an alarm.

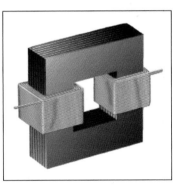

Transformer
A transformer changes the voltage. It is an iron frame with coils of wire wound around it. Electrical energy is supplied to the transformer by the primary coil. This coil creates a magnetic field, which makes a current flow through the secondary coil. The voltage it produces depends on the amount of wire curled around each of the two coils.

A SIREN SOUNDS THE ALARM IF A BREAK-IN IS DETECTED.

Telephones

Telephones allow people to communicate with each other over long distances. A telephone does two jobs. First, when someone speaks into a telephone, it changes the sound of the voice into a vibrating electric current. Second, when a caller's voice arrives as an electric current, the telephone changes it back into sound waves. So, a telephone is really an energy converter. It changes sound energy into electrical energy and electrical energy into sound. A telephone must also be able to find and connect to one other telephone among all the millions of telephones in the world. For this, it has a keypad. To make a telephone call, a person enters a unique number that identifies the other telephone. High-speed computers connect the many millions of telephone calls made every day around the world.

Inside the handset
When you speak into a telephone mouthpiece (*right, above*), the sound waves from your voice cause vibrations in a thin disk called a diaphragm. The diaphragm makes an iron armature vibrate, too, which makes an electric current flow through a coil near a magnet. This current then travels down the telephone line to another telephone.

When an electrical current is received by an earpiece (*right*), it flows through coils of wire. Magnetic forces produced by the coils make a nearby magnet vibrate. The magnet is linked to a diaphragm, which then vibrates to make the sound waves of the caller's voice.

THE TELEPHONE HANDSET

MOUTHPIECE

THE VIBRATING DISK, OR DIAPHRAGM

A WIRE COIL MAKES AN ELECTRIC CURRENT WHEN THE ARMATURE VIBRATES.

SPEAKING INTO THE MOUTHPIECE MAKES A DIAPHRAGM AND AN ARMATURE VIBRATE.

THE TONE CALLER "RINGS" WHEN IT RECEIVES A CALL.

ELECTRIC CURRENTS FROM THE CALLER MAKE WIRE COILS PRODUCE MAGNETIC FORCES.

SOUND OUTLETS

MAGNETIC FORCES MAKE A MAGNET VIBRATE.

A FINE WIRE TRANSFERS THE MAGNET'S VIBRATIONS TO THE DIAPHRAGM, WHICH PRODUCES SOUND.

EARPIECE

The telephone

Most telephones consist of a handset, containing a microphone; an earpiece; and a base unit, containing a keypad and electronic circuits. Some types of telephones have screens that show the time and the number being dialed. Lifting the handset and dialing numbers on the keypad tells the computer at the nearest telephone exchange which line to connect the telephone to. Extra control buttons allow people to set the time on the display, adjust the loudness and tone of the ring, or dial the last number called by pressing one button.

A CABLE CONNECTS THE TELEPHONE TO THE NEAREST EXCHANGE.

A LIQUID-CRYSTAL DISPLAY SHOWS THE TIME AND NUMBERS DIALED.

Making a call

When you speak into a telephone, your voice is converted into an electrical current. The current is an electrical copy of your voice, which changes in time with your voice. The electrical current travels along the wire from your telephone to another telephone, which may be close or on the other side of the world. There, the electrical current is changed back into sound.

THE RINGING TONE CAN BE SWITCHED TO SOFT, LOUD, OR OFF.

THE KEYPAD IS MOUNTED ON ITS OWN CIRCUIT BOARD.

PRESSING A KEY CLOSES A SWITCH ON THE CIRCUIT BOARD BELOW.

BUTTONS CONTROL EXTRA FUNCTIONS BUILT INTO THE TELEPHONE.

ELECTRONIC COMPONENTS ARE LINKED BY METAL TRACKS.

COMPONENTS AND TRACKS FORM PATHWAYS ALONG WHICH ELECTRICAL CURRENTS FLOW.

THE "*" AND "#" KEYS CONTROL EXTRA FUNCTIONS.

Fax machines

Facsimile-transmission (fax) machines send documents long distances by telephone. Motorized rollers pull each page into the machine. A light shines on it, line by line. The reflections from the white parts of the paper are changed into coded electric signals. The signals are sent along a telephone line. At the other end, another fax machine uses the code to control a printer, which prints a copy of the original page, line by line (*below*).

Telephone Networks

Telephones all around the world are linked together in a very complicated global network. Cables, optical fibers, radio links, and space satellites send millions of telephone calls back and forth every day.

In the past, telephone calls were connected by human operators using hand-controlled switchboards. Today, the telephone network is so large and complex that computers connect telephone calls.

All telephones were once installed in one place and connected to a telephone line by cable. Now, there are mobile phones that are small enough to slip into a pocket. These phones are linked to the telephone network by radio. People on ships at sea or flying in airplanes can make calls using satellite telephones. Solar-powered telephones allow people to communicate from remote parts of the world where there are no main power supplies.

COMMUNICATIONS SATELLITES ORBIT HIGH ABOVE EVERY CONTINENT.

RADIO SIGNALS SENT UP TO A SATELLITE ARE CALLED THE UPLINK.

SIGNALS SENT DOWN FROM A SATELLITE ARE CALLED THE DOWNLINK.

MOST COMMUNICATIONS SIGNALS TRAVEL UNDERGROUND OR BY RADIO, BUT SOME STILL TRAVEL ALONG WIRES ON POLES.

MICROWAVES CARRY COMMUNICATIONS SIGNALS OVER LONG DISTANCES WITHOUT CABLES.

INSIDE A COMPUTERIZED TELEPHONE EXCHANGE

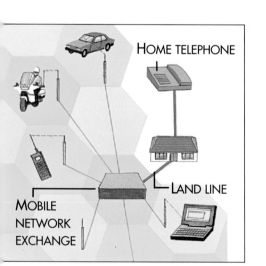

HOME TELEPHONE

LAND LINE

MOBILE NETWORK EXCHANGE

Mobile telephones

Areas where mobile telephones can be used are divided into a pattern of geographic cells. Each cell has a radio antenna that can communicate with mobile telephones within the cell. When a mobile phone moves from one cell to another in the middle of a call, the call is automatically switched to the next cell. Mobile networks are linked to the rest of the international telephone system by radio.

Telephone exchanges

Telephones are connected to telephone exchanges. Computers in automatic exchanges determine where each call is going and connect it to the correct telephone line. If it is a long-distance call, the local exchange connects it to another exchange. The computers work so fast that they can switch a call in one-millionth of a second.

DISH FARMS LINK COMMUNICATIONS CENTERS TO SATELLITES.

Satellites and cables

Communications satellites (1) allow airliners (2), military aircraft (3), and ships (4) to communicate with each other and with people on the ground. Telephone signals are transmitted from an airliner by radio. These are picked up by a satellite orbiting far above Earth and passed to a dish on the ground (5). Undersea cables (6) still carry many thousands of telephone calls between different continents.

MICROWAVES TRAVEL IN A STRAIGHT LINE FROM ONE DISH TO ANOTHER.

MICROWAVE DISHES ARE MOUNTED ON TOP OF TALL TOWERS SO THAT THEY CAN "SEE" FARTHER.

OUR WORLD IS CRISSCROSSED BY INVISIBLE RADIO SIGNALS CARRYING COUNTLESS TELEPHONE CALLS.

SUBMARINE TELEPHONE CABLES WERE ONCE METAL, BUT NOW THEY ARE OPTICAL FIBER CABLES.

Optical cables

Metal telephone cables, which carry telephone calls as electric currents, are being replaced by optical fiber cables. Optical cables carry telephone calls as streams of light flashes that travel along fine glass threads. The light reflects along the fiber's core. Optical cables can carry many more telephone calls than metal cables. A pencil-thin optical cable containing 100 fibers can carry up to 500,000 conversations traveling at the speed of light.

CORE

OPTICAL FIBER

LIGHT BEAM

ONE SUBMARINE (UNDERSEA) TELEPHONE CABLE CAN CARRY 500,000 TELEPHONE CALLS.

SUBMARINE TELEPHONE CABLES ARE LAID BY SHIPS WITH SPECIAL EQUIPMENT.

Satellites

Communications satellites are spacecraft that beam radio signals around the world. These signals might be telephone calls, television programs, or computer data. All sorts of information can be changed into radio signals and sent anywhere on Earth. The information travels at the speed of light in a fraction of a second. One communications satellite can handle tens of thousands of telephone calls. Radio signals sent from Earth into space are received by the satellite and then transmitted back down to Earth again. Radio equipment on a satellite needs electricity to work, so communications satellites have solar panels to make the electricity. They also have small rocket thrusters to keep them in the correct position with their antennae always pointing to Earth. If a satellite begins to drift out of position, the thrusters move it back again.

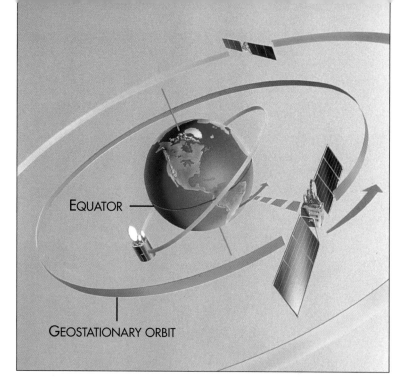

EQUATOR

GEOSTATIONARY ORBIT

Geostationary orbit

Satellites flying close to Earth have to fly very fast to stop gravity from pulling them back down. Gravity is weaker farther away from Earth, so satellites there can move more slowly. Most communications satellites circle Earth 22,370 miles (36,000 km) above the equator, an imaginary line around Earth's middle. A satellite in this special orbit, called a geostationary orbit, circles Earth once every twenty-four hours. Since Earth also turns once every twenty-four hours, the satellite always seems to be at the same point in the sky.

AN ANTENNA ON EARTH SENDS RADIO SIGNALS UP TO THE SATELLITE.

RADIO SIGNALS TRAVEL IN A STRAIGHT LINE THROUGH THE AIR AND THEN THROUGH SPACE TO THE SATELLITE.

RADIO SIGNALS RETURN TO EARTH.

SUNLIGHT STRIKES THE SOLAR PANELS.

SOLAR CELLS MAKE ELECTRICITY.

FUEL TANK FOR THE
ROCKET ENGINE

THRUSTER

THE SATELLITE IS
MOVED BY FIRING
ITS MAIN ROCKET.

RADIO RECEIVERS
AND TRANSMITTERS

SOLAR PANELS UNFOLD FROM
THE SIDES OF THE SATELLITE
AFTER IT IS LAUNCHED. EACH
PANEL HAS THOUSANDS OF
SOLAR CELLS.

THESE WIDE REFLECTORS
SPREAD OUT A RADIO BEAM
SO THAT THE SIGNALS CAN
BE RECEIVED ACROSS AN
ENTIRE COUNTRY.

SOLAR PANELS CHANGE
SUNLIGHT INTO ELECTRICITY
TO PROVIDE POWER FOR THE
SATELLITE'S RADIO EQUIPMENT.

SMALL DISH-SHAPED RADIO
ANTENNAE RECEIVE SIGNALS
FROM EARTH AND SEND THEM
BACK AGAIN.

COMMUNICATIONS SATELLITES
ARE FITTED WITH DIFFERENT
TYPES OF RADIO ANTENNAE
TO HANDLE DIFFERENT
RADIO SIGNALS.

Solar power

Communications satellites
must work in space for
many years. During that
time, they have to make
their own electricity. The
electricity is made by solar
cells. When light hits a
solar cell, the cell behaves
like a tiny battery and
makes a small amount
of electricity. Thousands
of cells work together to
make enough electricity
to power the satellite's
onboard equipment.

Communications dish

Radio signals from satellites
in space are received on
Earth by dish-shaped
antennae. The signals are
very weak. A dish-shaped
antenna strengthens them
by collecting signals over
a large area and then
bringing them together
in one small spot where
the receiver is. The radio
receiver may be held above
the dish at the end of one
or more legs, or it may be
behind a hole in the middle
of the dish.

RADIO SIGNALS
FROM A SATELLITE

MOTORS TURN AND
TILT THE DISH.

Radios

A radio set receives radio signals and changes them into sounds. First, an antenna picks up the signals. The antenna might be a length of wire, a coil of wire, or a long metal rod. Invisible radio waves streaming past the antenna make tiny electric currents flow inside the antenna. The radio set changes and amplifies (strengthens) these tiny currents so that they can make a loudspeaker work. Radio signals vibrate very quickly. They vibrate about 100 million times per second for a Very High Frequency (VHF) radio program. These signals "carry" the sound signals. A radio set separates the sound signals from the radio signals and changes them into sound.

A radio antenna picks up dozens, perhaps hundreds, of radio stations. People select just one station to listen to by turning a tuning dial or pressing a button.

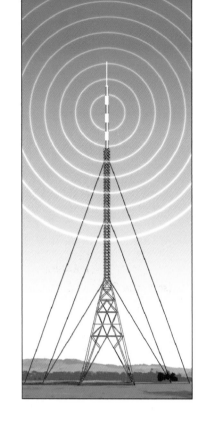

Radio transmitters
Radio-transmitting antennae broadcast radio signals in all directions. Antennae are often on top of tall towers, which are built on high ground. A large radio transmitter serving a wide area is very powerful. It may be equivalent to the power of 250 kilowatts.

PEOPLE TURN THE TUNING DIAL TO TUNE IN TO DIFFERENT RADIO STATIONS.

A NEEDLE ON A SCALE OR SOMETIMES A DIGITAL DISPLAY SHOWS TO WHICH STATION THE RADIO IS TUNED.

THE RADIO CIRCUIT IS MADE OF COMPONENTS ATTACHED TO A PRINTED CIRCUIT BOARD.

Microphones
Microphones broadcast sound on the radio, such as a newscaster's voice. A microphone changes sound waves into an electrical current flowing along a wire. The sound waves make a thin disk called a diaphragm vibrate. The diaphragm is attached to a coil of wire inside a magnet. When the diaphragm moves, the coil moves, too, and the magnet creates tiny electrical currents in the coil. The electrical currents change and vibrate in the same patterns as the sound waves.

A FOAM WINDSCREEN STOPS THE WIND FROM MAKING RUSHING NOISES.

SOUNDS PASS THROUGH THE WINDSCREEN AND MAKE THE DIAPHRAGM VIBRATE.

FIXED MAGNET

A MAGNET MAKES ELECTRICAL CURRENTS FLOW IN A COIL OF THIN WIRE THAT VIBRATES WITH THE DIAPHRAGM.

WIRES CARRY THE ELECTRICAL CURRENTS AWAY.

PORTABLE RADIOS ARE POWERED BY BATTERIES THAT FIT INSIDE A BATTERY COMPARTMENT.

A TELESCOPIC ANTENNA IS MADE FROM METAL TUBES THAT SLIDE INSIDE EACH OTHER.

FM RADIO STATIONS ARE RECEIVED BY A TELESCOPIC ANTENNA.

A SWITCH SELECTS ONE OUT OF TWO OR MORE DIFFERENT WAVE BANDS (*see page 33*).

THE VOLUME-CONTROL DIAL

BUTTONS CAN BE PROGRAMMED SO THAT SELECTED STATIONS CAN BE TUNED IN QUICKLY.

The loudspeaker

A loudspeaker changes electric currents into sounds. Speakers work like microphones in reverse. The main difference between them is size. The loudspeaker has a larger magnet than a microphone. It also has a large cone instead of a tiny diaphragm because it has to push all the air in front of it to make sound waves.

In a loudspeaker, a changing electric current flows through a coil next to a magnet, which makes the coil vibrate. The coil is attached to a large cone that then vibrates. The vibrating cone sends out pressure waves, which we hear as sounds.

THE LOUDSPEAKER CHANGES ELECTRICAL SIGNALS INTO SOUND WAVES.

COILS OF WIRE AROUND A METAL ROD RECEIVE AM RADIO SIGNALS.

SOUND ESCAPES FROM THE LOUDSPEAKER THROUGH HOLES OR SLOTS IN A GRILL.

THE SIGNAL FROM THE RADIO FLOWS THROUGH A COIL NEAR A MAGNET AND MAKES THE LOUDSPEAKER'S CONE VIBRATE.

THE VIBRATING LOUDSPEAKER CONE PUSHES SOUND WAVES OUT.

Radio Waves

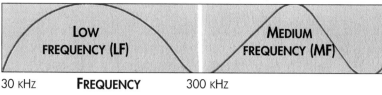

6.2 MILES (10 KM)	**WAVELENGTH**	0.6 MILES (1 KM)
LOW FREQUENCY (LF)		**MEDIUM FREQUENCY (MF)**
30 KHZ	**FREQUENCY**	300 KHZ

R adio waves are invisible waves of energy that travel through the air. We use radio waves mainly for communicating with each other. Both radio and television sets rely on radio waves to carry their sound and picture signals. In radio transmission, a microphone changes sound into electrical signals. These signals are combined with a radio wave called a carrier wave and then transmitted. When received, the signals are separated from the carrier wave, amplified to make them stronger, and then fed into a loudspeaker. There are many different kinds of radio waves. Some radio waves stay close to Earth's surface as they travel along. Others bounce off a layer of charged particles in the atmosphere called the ionosphere. Some radio waves pass into space and are used to communicate with satellites and astronauts.

COMMUNICATIONS SATELLITES RELAY RADIO SIGNALS FROM ONE PART OF EARTH TO ANOTHER.

RADIO WAVES BETWEEN 0.3 INCHES (8 MM) AND 33 FEET (10 M) LONG PASS THROUGH THE IONOSPHERE.

THE IONOSPHERE REFLECTS SOME RADIO SIGNALS — BACK TO EARTH.

THE RADIO SIGNALS SENT TO EARTH BY A SATELLITE ARE CALLED THE DOWNLINK.

THE LONGEST RADIO WAVES HUG EARTH'S SURFACE.

THE RADIO SIGNALS SENT UP TO A SATELLITE ARE CALLED THE UPLINK.

A DISH-SHAPED ANTENNA TRANSMITS A CONCENTRATED RADIO BEAM.

SUBMARINES CAN COMMUNICATE BY RAISING A RADIO ANTENNA ABOVE THE WATER

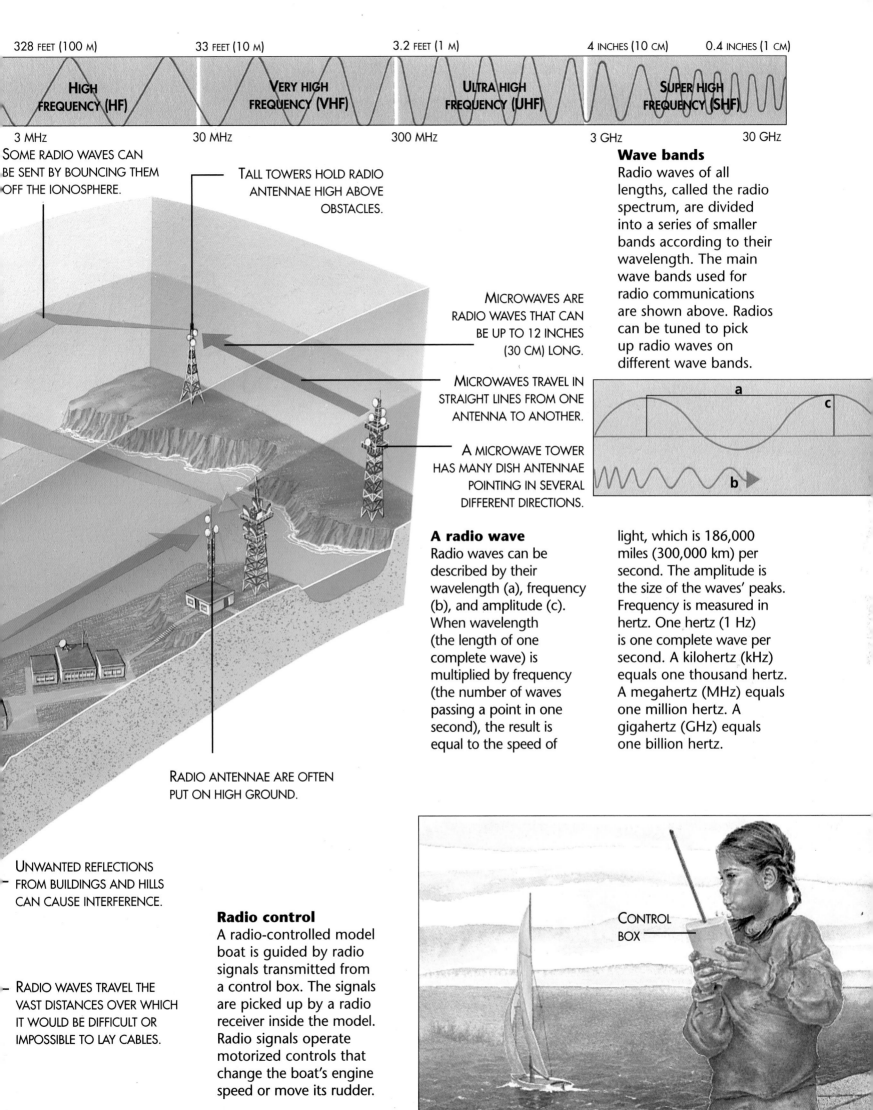

328 FEET (100 M)	33 FEET (10 M)	3.2 FEET (1 M)	4 INCHES (10 CM)	0.4 INCHES (1 CM)
HIGH FREQUENCY (HF)	**VERY HIGH FREQUENCY (VHF)**	**ULTRA HIGH FREQUENCY (UHF)**	**SUPER HIGH FREQUENCY (SHF)**	
3 MHz	30 MHz	300 MHz	3 GHz	30 GHz

SOME RADIO WAVES CAN BE SENT BY BOUNCING THEM OFF THE IONOSPHERE.

TALL TOWERS HOLD RADIO ANTENNAE HIGH ABOVE OBSTACLES.

MICROWAVES ARE RADIO WAVES THAT CAN BE UP TO 12 INCHES (30 CM) LONG.

MICROWAVES TRAVEL IN STRAIGHT LINES FROM ONE ANTENNA TO ANOTHER.

A MICROWAVE TOWER HAS MANY DISH ANTENNAE POINTING IN SEVERAL DIFFERENT DIRECTIONS.

RADIO ANTENNAE ARE OFTEN PUT ON HIGH GROUND.

UNWANTED REFLECTIONS FROM BUILDINGS AND HILLS CAN CAUSE INTERFERENCE.

RADIO WAVES TRAVEL THE VAST DISTANCES OVER WHICH IT WOULD BE DIFFICULT OR IMPOSSIBLE TO LAY CABLES.

Wave bands

Radio waves of all lengths, called the radio spectrum, are divided into a series of smaller bands according to their wavelength. The main wave bands used for radio communications are shown above. Radios can be tuned to pick up radio waves on different wave bands.

A radio wave

Radio waves can be described by their wavelength (a), frequency (b), and amplitude (c). When wavelength (the length of one complete wave) is multiplied by frequency (the number of waves passing a point in one second), the result is equal to the speed of light, which is 186,000 miles (300,000 km) per second. The amplitude is the size of the waves' peaks. Frequency is measured in hertz. One hertz (1 Hz) is one complete wave per second. A kilohertz (kHz) equals one thousand hertz. A megahertz (MHz) equals one million hertz. A gigahertz (GHz) equals one billion hertz.

Radio control

A radio-controlled model boat is guided by radio signals transmitted from a control box. The signals are picked up by a radio receiver inside the model. Radio signals operate motorized controls that change the boat's engine speed or move its rudder.

CONTROL BOX

Radar

Radar is a system that uses radio waves to find distant objects, from storm clouds to aircraft. A radar transmitter sends out pulses of radio waves. If the radio waves hit an object, some bounce back, and this reflection is picked up by a receiver. Metal objects, such as aircraft or ships, produce the strongest radar reflections. People can calculate how far away an object is by using the time it takes for a radar pulse to return to the receiver. This type of radar is called primary radar. Secondary radar is another type of radar that works in a different way.

Secondary radar triggers a radio set to send out information. When an airplane device called a transponder receives secondary radar pulses, it transmits a radio signal containing coded information about the aircraft. The latest military aircraft, called stealth aircraft, are designed to produce the smallest possible radar reflection, which makes them difficult for radar to detect.

Secondary radar
Air-traffic controllers use radar to guide aircraft safely to a destination. They need to identify individual aircraft on their radar screens, see how high the aircraft are flying, and confirm their destinations. Every aircraft carries a transponder, which supplies air-traffic controllers with this information. When an aircraft's transponder receives the correct radar signal, it transmits the aircraft's flight number along with its height and planned destination.

THE TRANSPONDER SENDS INFORMATION ABOUT THE AIRCRAFT TO AIR-TRAFFIC CONTROLLERS.

AIRCRAFT CANNOT CHANGE HEIGHT OR DIRECTION WITHOUT PERMISSION FROM AIR-TRAFFIC CONTROLLERS.

RADAR SIGNALS

SECONDARY RADAR ASKS THE AIRCRAFT'S TRANSPONDER TO IDENTIFY ITSELF.

THE RADAR ANTENNA ROTATES TO PICK UP SIGNALS FROM AIRCRAFT IN EVERY DIRECTION.

A TOWER HOLDS THE RADAR ANTENNA ABOVE NEARBY OBSTRUCTIONS.

RADAR BEAMS BOUNCE OFF STORM CLOUDS.

WEATHER RADAR SCANS THE SKY AHEAD.

THE WEATHER RADAR DISH IS INSIDE THE AIRCRAFT'S NOSE.

THE AIRPLANE'S FLIGHT-DECK WEATHER SCREEN

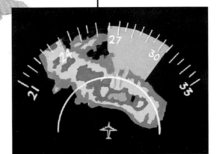

Weather radar

An aircraft's nose contains a small radar dish that scans the sky ahead of the aircraft. This radar detects moisture in the air. The information it receives appears on a small screen on the aircraft's flight deck (*left*). The pilot uses the weather radar to avoid storms. Blustery winds could make the flight uncomfortably rough for passengers, and lightning is also a danger because it could damage the aircraft. Storms show up clearly because of the heavy rain they contain.

PRIMARY RADAR ANTENNA

Air-traffic control

An air-traffic controller's radar screen (*right*) shows the positions of all aircraft within range. Each aircraft on the screen has a call sign, the code name that air-traffic controllers use to talk to the pilot, and a second code showing the aircraft's height and the airport that is its destination.

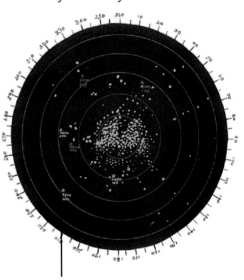

CODES IDENTIFY DIFFERENT AIRCRAFT.

PRIMARY RADAR LOCATES THE AIRCRAFT.

Calculators

A calculator is a machine designed to do arithmetic. In the past, calculating machines were big, hand-operated mechanisms with toothed wheels, levers, and dials. Today, calculators can be as small as a credit card, and they can do complicated calculations in less than a second because they work electronically. A battery or solar panel supplies the electrical current. The machine calculates by processing pulses of electricity inside a microchip. The electric pulses represent numbers. All calculators are programmed to perform four basic tasks: addition, subtraction, multiplication, and division. Many calculators can do extra calculations, such as finding the square root of a number. Some can do very complicated scientific calculations. Most have an extra electronic memory for storing numbers that are frequently used. A few calculators have a built-in printer that prints all the numbers entered and the results of calculations.

Inside a calculator
An electronic calculator contains a circuit board. Metal strips on the circuit board link all the chips and other components with the battery, keys, and display. Pressing a key closes a switch underneath it and completes an electric circuit, sending a series of electric pulses to the calculator's microchips. A memory chip stores the pulses, and a processor chip does the calculations.

LIQUID-CRYSTAL DISPLAY

A WIDE, FLAT "RIBBON" CABLE CONNECTS THE DISPLAY TO THE CIRCUIT BOARD.

THE DISPLAY-DRIVER CHIP CONTROLS THE DISPLAY.

THE CENTRAL-PROCESSOR CHIP DOES ALL THE CALCULATIONS.

THE CHIPS ARE CONNECTED TO THE CIRCUIT BOARD BY METAL TERMINALS ALONG THE EDGES OF THE CHIPS.

RESISTORS AND OTHER ELECTRONIC COMPONENTS CONTROL THE ELECTRIC CURRENTS FLOWING THROUGH THE CALCULATOR.

TRANSISTORS SWITCH ELECTRIC CURRENTS FROM CHIP TO CHIP.

Making microchips
A pure silicon crystal is cut into thin slices called wafers. Dozens of chips are made on each wafer by adding about twenty extra layers of chemicals in some places and etching away the surface chemicals and silicone in others. Each wafer is cut into separate tiny chips that are sealed into plastic blocks for protection.

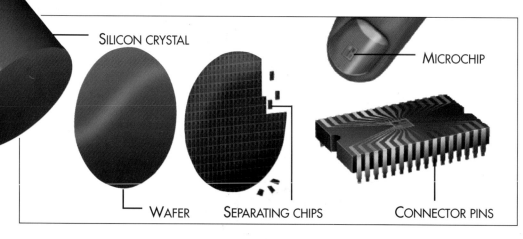

SILICON CRYSTAL

MICROCHIP

WAFER   SEPARATING CHIPS   CONNECTOR PINS

SEVEN-SEGMENT DISPLAY

SEGMENTS THAT ARE SWITCHED ON TURN BLACK.

NARROW TRACKS CARRY A VOLTAGE TO SOME DISPLAY SEGMENTS.

Liquid numbers

Any number can be made with only seven lines, or segments, arranged in a figure "8." The display is made from two sheets of glass with a special substance called liquid crystal between them. Normally, it works like a mirror. Light passes through it and bounces out again from a shiny backing. When a segment is turned on by the calculator, the liquid crystal twists the light. It is not reflected back, and the segment goes dark.

THE LIQUID-CRYSTAL SCREEN CONTAINS A ROW OF SEVEN SEGMENT DISPLAYS.

AN ADVANCED CALCULATOR MAY HAVE DOZENS OF KEYS FOR DIFFERENT TYPES OF CALCULATIONS.

In and out

All electronic calculators have an input device (the keypad), a processor, and an output device (the display). Information is fed into the calculator's memory by pressing keys. The processor chip takes the numbers stored in the memory and does the calculation. A fraction of a second later, the answer is sent to the display.

PRESSING A KEY OPERATES A SWITCH UNDERNEATH IT.

FUNCTION KEYS TELL THE CALCULATOR WHAT TO DO.

DECIMAL POINT KEY

KEYED IN NUMBERS AND ANSWERS ARE SENT TO THE DISPLAY.

PRESSING THE "EQUALS" KEY TELLS THE CALCULATOR TO DO THE CALCULATION AND SHOW THE ANSWER.

MEMORY CHIPS STORE NUMBERS UNTIL THEY ARE NEEDED FOR A CALCULATION.

PRESSING KEYS INPUTS INFORMATION.

THE PROCESSOR DOES THE CALCULATIONS.

Computers

A computer is an electronic machine that takes in information and changes it by following a set of instructions called a program. Computer programs are also called software, and the computer machinery is called hardware. Computers have four basic parts: input, memory, processor, and output. The input device, such as a keyboard, feeds instructions and data into the computer. The computer's memory then holds the information until it is needed. Software tells the processor what to do with the data, and the results appear on an output device, such as a screen. The contents of the memory disappear when a computer is switched off, so important information is kept by recording it on a hard disk in the computer.

Computer monitor

A computer screen works in the same way as a television screen. The picture is made of thousands of tiny points of light. Each point may be red, green, or blue. Any color can be made by mixing these three basic light colors. The computer controls which colors appear at which points on the screen.

A COMPUTER CAN CREATE THREE-DIMENSIONAL PICTURES, EVEN THOUGH THE SCREEN IS ALMOST FLAT.

USING ONLY THREE BASIC COLORS, A COMPUTER CAN PRODUCE ANY COLOR OR SHADE OF THE RAINBOW.

Disks

Three main types of disks are used to store computer programs and data. Floppy disks and hard disks are magnetic. The third, the CD-ROM, is like a music CD. A personal computer may use all three types.

DATA CAN BE COPIED ONTO A FLOPPY DISK.

THE KEYS ARE CONNECTED TO METAL STRIPS ON A BOARD CALLED A PRINTED CIRCUIT BOARD.

ONE WAY OF PUTTING INFORMATION INTO A COMPUTER IS TO TYPE IT ON THE KEYBOARD.

A CD-ROM IS A COMPACT DISC THAT HOLDS INFORMATION FOR READING ONLY.

A FLOPPY DISK IS USED BY PUSHING IT INTO THE COMPUTER HERE.

PRESSING A KEY COMPLETES A CIRCUIT AND SENDS AN ELECTRICAL SIGNAL TO THE COMPUTER.

The microprocessor

A microprocessor is a computer's master control chip. It is also called the central processing unit (CPU). All types of data are stored inside a computer as tiny pulses of electricity. The microprocessor controls where these pulses go and what they do. A clock controls how fast the microprocessor works. Computers work very quickly because their clocks tick millions of times per second.

CHIP

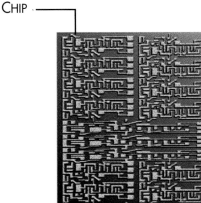

CHIPS ARE CONNECTED TO THE REST OF THE COMPUTER BY METAL TERMINALS (PINS).

THE CHIP CONTAINS THOUSANDS OF TINY ELECTRONIC COMPONENTS.

INFORMATION IS STORED IN RANDOM-ACCESS MEMORY (RAM) CHIPS ONLY WHILE THE COMPUTER IS SWITCHED ON.

A FAN KEEPS THE COMPUTER'S CIRCUITS COOL.

The mouse

People can use a device called a mouse to control a computer. When a mouse is moved, a directional pointer on the computer screen moves, too. People move a mouse so that the pointer selects something on the screen. Then people press a button on the mouse to send instructions telling the computer what to do.

THE MICROPROCESSOR IS A COMPUTER'S MASTER CONTROL CHIP.

A BALL UNDERNEATH A MOUSE ROLLS WHEN THE MOUSE IS MOVED.

A COMPUTER MOUSE USUALLY HAS TWO CONTROL BUTTONS TO CLICK.

A HARD DISK STORES INFORMATION LIKE A FLOPPY DISK, BUT A HARD DISK CANNOT BE TAKEN OUT OF THE COMPUTER.

A SMALL LOUDSPEAKER CAN MAKE SOUNDS.

THE BALL TURNS WHEELS, WHICH TELL THE COMPUTER THAT THE MOUSE IS MOVING.

THE MOUSE

Peripherals

Computer equipment includes the computer itself and all the other machines and devices that are connected to it. Pieces of equipment connected to computers are called peripherals. Peripherals include monitors, printers, modems, and scanners. A computer's monitor is the screen that shows what the computer is doing. A printer turns stored information in the computer's memory into printed documents. A modem connects a computer to a telephone line so that it can communicate with other computers. Modem is short for modulator / demodulator. A scanner changes a picture or printed text into computer data in a process called digitization. As computer data, the picture or text can be changed, stored, copied, and printed out.

Scanners

To feed a picture into a computer, the picture is placed facedown on the glass plate in a scanner. The cover closes over the picture. A bright light shines through the glass onto the paper. What is printed on the paper determines how bright its reflection is. A motor moves the scan head, which contains the light, down the length of the paper. It uses a system of mirrors and lenses to relay the reflections onto light sensors. Sometimes light sensors are built

LIGHT SENSORS CHANGE LIGHT REFLECTED FROM THE PAPER INTO AN ELECTRIC SIGNAL.

MIRRORS AND LENSES DIRECT REFLECTIONS ONTO LIGHT SENSORS.

AN ELECTRONIC CIRCUIT CHANGES THE ELECTRIC SIGNAL INTO COMPUTER DATA.

THE DOCUMENT TO BE SCANNED IS PLACED ON A GLASS PLATE.

THE SCAN HEAD MOVES DOWN THE PAPER, LIGHTING IT UP LINE BY LINE.

Changing pictures

An image that has been scanned into a computer can be completely changed. Using a design or illustration program, people can change the color, shape, and size of all or part of any image. For example, this scanned photograph has been changed. The zebra's stripes were altered to make it more colorful.

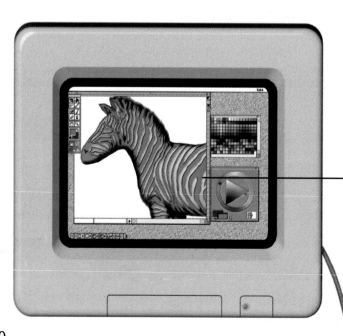

EVERY POINT IN THE SCANNED PICTURE CAN BE CHANGED BY A COMPUTER.

into the scan head itself. The light sensors convert the reflections into electrical signals. The reflection's brightness determines the strength of the signals. These signals are changed into electrical pulses that are sent to the main computer.

A FLEXIBLE RIBBON CABLE LINKS THE SCAN HEAD TO THE SCANNER.

CLEAN PAPER IS FED INTO THE LASER PRINTER.

A RULER SCALE SHOWS WHERE TO POSITION THE DOCUMENT.

A LID COVERS THE DOCUMENT TO KEEP OUT UNWANTED LIGHT.

THE RUBBER BELT DRIVES THE SCAN HEAD DOWN THE PAPER.

AN ELECTRIC MOTOR DRIVES A TOOTHED RUBBER BELT.

THE SCANNER COMMUNICATES WITH A COMPUTER THROUGH A CABLE AND DATA CONNECTOR.

Laser printers

Data sent by the computer to a laser printer turns a laser on and off. The laser produces a thin beam of light (1). A spinning mirror (2) reflects the beam onto an electrically-charged drum (3). The charge changes wherever light falls on the drum. Black toner powder sticks to parts of the drum, according to its charge pattern. Paper is pressed against the drum and takes up the toner (4). Finally, heated rollers glue the toner to the paper (5).

Modems

A modem changes computer data into electric signals that can be sent down a telephone line. At the other end of the line, another modem changes the signals back into computer data, which is fed into a second computer.

TELEPHONE LINE   A MODEM

Using Computers

Computers can store, process, and manipulate all sorts of information. The electrical pulses that travel through their amazingly complicated circuits may represent numbers, letters, sounds, or pictures. Computers can process this information millions of times faster than humans. Because of this, these machines have become an essential part of almost every type of industry and business. They are also very popular in the home. Their many uses include controlling machines, monitoring complex power and transport systems, managing global communications, providing access to vast amounts of information, and playing exciting computer games. They have also become very important in the television and motion-picture industry because of their ability to create or change lifelike pictures.

A COMPUTER SYSTEM IN A MODERN RAILWAY CONTROL CENTER

Controlling trains

The control center for a modern railway system relies heavily on computers. Sensors along the tracks feed information to the control center, which tells the computers where trains are and how the signals and switch points are set. The information appears as lights on a map of the railway network and on computer screens. Using the same computers, controllers can send out commands to change the switch points and railway signals.

THE COMPUTER GIVES THE SMOOTH SURFACES TEXTURE BY ADDING DETAIL, LIGHT, AND SHADE.

Creating characters

The first stage in creating a computerized, or virtual, character is building a clay model (1). The model is covered by a grid of lines. The points where lines cross are entered into the computer. A copy of the grid, called a wire frame, appears on the screen (2). The computer changes the wire frame into a solid figure (3) by filling in the surfaces. Finally, the figure is animated, or made to move, and given different expressions (4).

A COMPUTER CHARACTER BEGINS AS A 3-D CLAY MODEL.

(1)

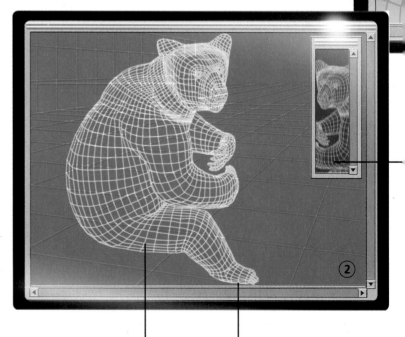

(2)

THE CHARACTER APPEARS ON THE COMPUTER SCREEN AS A SEE-THROUGH WIRE FRAME.

THE CHARACTER'S SHAPE IS EDITED AND CHANGED UNTIL IT LOOKS EXACTLY RIGHT.

THE CHARACTER IS ADDED TO A BACKGROUND.

FACIAL EXPRESSIONS ARE STORED IN THE COMPUTER'S MEMORY.

COLORS FOR THE CHARACTER ARE SELECTED FROM A COLOR PALETTE ON THE SCREEN.

④

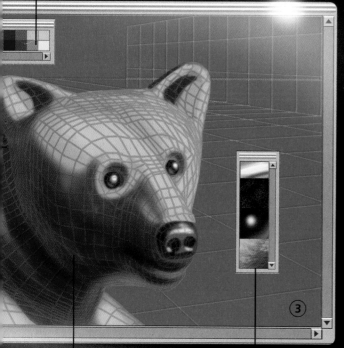

③

DIFFERENT EXPRESSIONS ARE PRODUCED BY MOVING CERTAIN POINTS ON THE CHARACTER'S FACE.

THE BACKGROUND MAY HAVE BEEN PHOTOGRAPHED, CREATED BY COMPUTER, OR PAINTED BY HAND.

A COMPUTER CONTROLS THE ROBOT ARM.

A WELDING TOOL HAS BEEN FITTED TO THE END OF THE ROBOT'S ARM.

THE WIRE FRAME IS FILLED IN BY THE COMPUTER TO FORM SOLID-LOOKING SURFACES.

THE COMPUTER PROGRAM CAN MIMIC A WIDE RANGE OF DIFFERENT SURFACE DETAILS.

THE CHARACTER CAN BE TURNED AROUND AND VIEWED FROM ANY ANGLE.

Robots

The movements of the robot arms that build many cars today are controlled by computers. First, the robot's computer is programmed with the necessary arm movements. The robot will then repeat the same series of movements until it is turned off or reprogrammed.

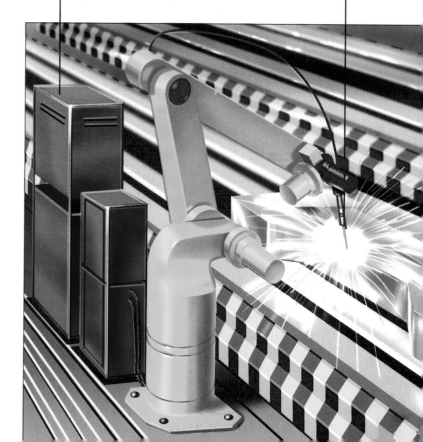

Computer Networks

Computer networks are groups of computers that can communicate with each other and exchange information. One problem faced by scientists trying to use early computers was that the computers were not always in the right place. A computer in one place often contained programs or information needed by scientists working somewhere else. There was no way of moving the programs or information to where they were needed. The problem was solved by connecting computers together to form a network. To begin with, only scientists could use networks. However, once computers were connected to telephone lines, it became much easier to form bigger networks that covered longer distances. Businesses linked computer networks together. But the most exciting development was connecting small computers to the biggest computers in the world, so everyone could use the super-fast computing power and vast memories of super-computers.

SEVERAL COMPUTERS ARE LINKED TOGETHER TO FORM A LOCAL AREA NETWORK (LAN).

NETWORKS ARE LINKED TO EACH OTHER THROUGH DEVICES CALLED ROUTERS.

TWO OR MORE LANS CONNECTED TOGETHER FORM A WIDE AREA NETWORK (WAN).

A CONNECTION TO A LAN IN ANOTHER BUILDING.

ELECTRONIC MESSAGES TRAVEL FROM COMPUTER TO COMPUTER AS E-MAIL.

A FILE SERVER HOLDS ALL THE MESSAGES IN ONE PLACE FOR COLLECTION.

World Wide Web

The best known computer network is the Internet. This international network of computers allows anyone with an ordinary home computer to link up with other computers all around the world. The home computer must first be linked to a telephone line by a modem. The modem changes computer data into a form that can be sent down a telephone line. It also converts any information received by telephone back into computer data. One of the Internet's most exciting and useful features is the World Wide Web. It enables anyone to move effortlessly among the millions of pages of information held in thousands of computers in different countries of the world.

A SERVICE PROVIDER'S COMPUTER SUPPLIES INTERNET SERVICES.

COMPUTERS AT A SERVICE PROVIDER COMMUNICATE WITH THE INTERNET.

THE SERVICE PROVIDER'S MODEM CHANGES ELECTRIC WAVES BACK INTO PULSES.

THIS HOME COMPUTER IS LINKED TO A MODEM.

ELECTRIC WAVES TRAVEL ALONG TELEPHONE LINES.

A MODEM CHANGES COMPUTER DATA INTO ELECTRIC WAVES.

Networks

Computers are often linked together so people can share the same information and machines, such as printers. The computer programs and data used by the network are stored in a central device called a file server. A small network is called a Local Area Network (LAN). Two or more LANs can be linked together to form a larger network called a Wide Area Network (WAN). Electronic messages, or e-mail, can be sent from one computer to any other computer in the same network (*see left*).

Global connections

Small networks of computers, including home computers, are connected to bigger networks. These are connected to even bigger networks of more powerful new computers, forming a global super-network of computers. The biggest, fastest, and most powerful computers are super-computers, which are linked together by high-speed information highways.

A CONNECTION TO THE INTERNET.

A CORE NETWORK OF SUPER-COMPUTERS

HIGH-SPEED INFORMATION HIGHWAYS

TELEPHONE LINKS BETWEEN COMPUTERS

SATELLITES LINK SUPER-COMPUTERS TOGETHER.

Glossary

amplifier: a device that makes electronic signals into louder and stronger sounds.

amplitude: the size of a radio wave's peaks.

aperture: a hole that can be opened or closed behind a camera lens to control the amount of light that shines onto the film.

capacitor: an electronic device that can store electrical current and help regulate its flow.

Charge-Coupled Device (CCD): a light-sensitive microchip that changes light into electricity inside a television camera.

circuit: the complete path of an electrical current, including the current's source.

coaxial cable: a cable with a metal core, a layer of insulation, and another ring of metal cable.

compact disc: a small, silvery disc that stores information to be read by using a laser beam.

current: the flow of electricity through a wire.

digitization: to electrically encode information, pictures, or sounds in a pattern of numbers.

electronics: devices that are powered by electrical currents made by electrons.

electrons: tiny, electrically charged particles that circle the center of an atom.

frequency: the number of radio waves passing a point in one second.

fuse: in electrical equipment, a safety device designed to cut off the power if too much electrical current flows through a circuit.

geostationary: at the same point above Earth.

grid: a protective metal plate with even spaces on it; a linked network of power suppliers or stations.

hard disk: a set of enclosed disks that stores information inside a computer.

information highway: the high-speed global communications network carrying voice, video, and information by satellite, cables, and radio.

laser: a device that makes a very narrow, powerful beam of light.

lens: a piece of curved glass or plastic in a camera; lenses collect and focus light.

microchip: a small piece of silicon with electronic circuits layered onto it.

monitor: the display screen of a computer or the television screen used in a studio to show what is being recorded or broadcast.

motion picture: a movie, or a series of still pictures recorded on a strip of film; the pictures are shown so quickly that they appear to move.

orbit: the path an object follows as it circles a larger object in space.

peripherals: pieces of equipment, such as printers, that are connected to a computer.

phosphors: chemical elements that glow in dark conditions.

printing press: a machine that prints words and designs by pressing paper on an inked surface.

prism: a block of glass that bends light or separates it into the colors of the spectrum.

radar: an instrument that locates distant objects by bouncing radio waves off them.

resistor: a device used to protect or control an electrical current.

satellite: a spacecraft that orbits Earth; satellites can receive and send radio signals.

shutter: the part of a camera that opens the aperture to let light in to reach the film.

software: a set of instructions that tells computers what to do; also called a program.

transformer: a device to change electrical current to a desired voltage and current.

transistor: a small block of material to control the flow of electrical current in equipment.

transmitter: a device that sends encoded radio or television signals.

voltage: the force that makes an electrical current flow; the strength of that force.

wavelength: the length of one complete radio wave.

More Books to Read

Click: Fun with Photography. Susanna Price and Tim Stephens (Sterling Publications)

Communication. Yesterday's Science, Today's Technology (series). Robert Gardner (Twenty-First Century Books)

The Computer Age. Modern Media (series). (Barron's Educational Series)

Computer Fun for Everyone: Great Things To Do and Make with Any Computer. Elin Kordahl Saltveit (John Wiley & Sons)

Computer Graphics & Animation. Computer Guides (series). Asha Kalbag and Russell Punter (Usborne)

Computers. Twentieth-Century Inventions (series). Steve Parker (Raintree Steck-Vaughn)

Film and Television. Twentieth-Century Inventions (series). Louise Wordsworth (Raintree Steck-Vaughn)

101 Things to Do With Your Computer. Usborne Computer Guides (series). Gillian Doherty and Philippa Wingate (EDC Publications)

Radio & Television. Worldwise (series). Peter Lafferty (Franklin Watts)

Television: What's Behind What You See. W. Carter Merbreier and Linda Capus Riley (Farrar Straus & Giroux)

Why Doesn't My Floppy Disk Flop? And Other Kids' Computer Questions Answered by the Compududes. Peter Cook and Scott Manning (John Wiley & Sons)

Videos

Computer Visions: A Fantastic Voyage Through the World of Computer Animation. (MPI Media Group)

Easy Photography. (Education 2000)

Know Your Camcorder Fundamentals. (TMW / Media Group)

Nerds 2.0.1: A Brief History of the Internet. (PBS Home Video)

Web Sites

American Museum of Photography
www.photographymuseum.com/

Animation by Pixar Animation Studios
www.pixar.com/funstuff/how-its-done.html

Cinema: How Are Hollywood Films Made?
www.learner.org/exhibits/cinema/

George Eastman House International Museum of Photography and Film
www.eastman.org/

Kids' Corner
www.media-awareness.ca/eng/med/kids/kindex.htm

Museum of Television
www.mztv.com/

The NoodleHead Videos
www.noodlehead.com/videos.htm

Oatmeal Box Pinhole Photography
www.nh.ultranet.com/~stewoody/

Some web sites stay current longer than others. For further web sites, use your search engines to locate the following topics: *animation, camera, circuit board, electrons, printing press, radar, radio waves,* and *satellite.*

Index